Write Now!
Get Your Book Out of Your Hea

It's said that everyone has a book inside t
to get that book on to the page. *Write No*
your ideas and turn them into a book. From finding time to write to
planning, structuring and editing, it guides you through the writing
process, helping you avoid common pitfalls.

This doesn't mean that your book will instantly attract a publisher, but
self-publishing means that's no longer the only way to become an author.
Write Now! includes ways to make your book more attractive to
publishers and readers, along with the pros and cons of different types of
publishing.

Writing a book is just one part of the process. Nowadays, promoting your
book is as important a part of being an author, whether you have a
publisher or not. *Write Now!* will steer you through the marketing
essentials to help you attract a bigger audience – and attention.

Write Now! will not teach you how to write: there are already plenty of
great books available that will help you hone your craft. Instead, it distills
my experiences writing 30 books for publishers including Penguin
Random-House, Carlton and Little Brown Book Group, into a brief guide
for people who want to get their book written and out into the world. I
can't promise to make you a publishing success – but I can help you finish
your book.

Contents

Introduction

Many people dream of becoming a writer. For some, it's about sharing their own story, or worlds they imagine. Others are fascinated by a subject area, or see being published as a pathway to riches. If you're one of the latter, you may want to buy a book on investment or sales instead – it's a lucky few who make a living out of writing, despite headlines about 'six figure advances'. However, if you want to write a book, *Write Now!* will help you get it on to the page and into the world.

I'm lucky enough to have had over 30 books published by major publishers in the UK and the US over the last couple of decades. I've also self-published several books for charity that made it into the Amazon top 10 charts. This has given me an insight into the realities of publishing. I'm often asked for advice on how to get started, so I decided to share what I've learned in *Write Now!*

At its core, writing a book entails typing one word after another, hence the book's title: there's a 100 percent chance of failure if your words stay inside your mind. However, getting readers for that book is another challenge. Making it readable is a start, but it takes a lot more than that to become a bestseller. *Write Now!* will help you give your book its best chance of success, offering a pithy guide to publishing.

Write Now! won't teach you how to write: there are plenty of books on that already, such as *Steering the Craft: A Twenty-First-Century Guide to Sailing the Sea of Story* by Ursula Le Guin, *The Writer's Journey* by Christopher Vogler and *On Writing* by Stephen King. However, it will take you through the process of writing a book, in a way that can be tailored to suit your life.

It's deliberately short so you don't need to spend hours reading before you start writing (though hopefully, you'll have spent hours reading already: a keen reader makes an informed writer.) With a little planning, your book has a lot better chance of success.

Planning

While the idea that a writer sits down at a blank page, types words that flow into their head and eventually ends up with a book is a romantic one, it's about as realistic as most romantic films. There may be some authors who write a book in this way, but planning makes the process a lot easier.

This is the stage where many writers get stuck. I've lost count of the number of people I've met who want to be writers but 'just need to do some more planning'. As with most major commitments in life, there will rarely be a 'perfect' time to start. It's about getting the balance right between planning and procrastination.

You don't need to know everything about your book before you start. Whether it's fiction or non-fiction, you'll find gaps as you go along, but you can continue researching after you've started writing. Getting words on a page gets you a lot closer to having a finished book than having folders full of research collated lovingly over years, and stored in a cupboard or folder on your hard drive.

Should You Write a Book?

However, there are some things that you need to plan before you start. The first of these is, 'should you write a book?' It's easy to have a 'brilliant' idea, only to discover that someone else has already written the book that you want to write.

While there's no rule saying a book has to be unique, your book will be much more saleable if it has a USP (Unique Selling Proposition). Maybe you're a leading expert in an area? Perhaps you have a different angle to everyone else writing about your subject, or have drawn inspiration from an original and noteworthy source? What is the core message of your book and why does it matter? Give people a reason to buy your book.

That's not to say you have to write your book with the objective of selling it. There are plenty of other reasons for writing books. You may want to:

- Capture your family history for future generations.
- Share your own memories to help future generations connect with you.
- Record a local place of interest.
- Use writing as therapy to deal with a traumatic experience.
- Preserve folklore or traditions in your local area.
- Write stories to tell your children.
- Explore your philosophical ideas in an ordered way.
- Provide a useful guide to a person, place or town for your local library.
- Get a story out of your head and onto a page.

If so, it's still a good idea to see what's out there. You may discover books that are useful for your own research, or authors who you'd like to cite in your book. However, your USP is less important if you're not planning on publishing your book.

Writing a book for your own pleasure and satisfaction can be just as valuable as publishing one. You may feel more able to be honest if you're writing the book without readers in mind, or feel more secure in your writing when you know it won't be judged by anyone else. With every book you write, you learn something new, so don't feel your book is any less important if you're writing it for yourself.

Has Someone Written Your Book?

If you *do* want to sell your book, start by doing an Amazon search for your potential title. If you're not sure what your title is, search for keywords around your book: if it's about fishing, search 'Fishing'. If it's a romance novel, check out the romance bestsellers' lists.

Has any book got the same name? While there's no copyright on titles, you don't want your book confused with others (any extra sales you generate from the confusion will almost certainly be matched by disgruntled reviews, negatively affecting future sales). If you're writing a romance, has your theme become a cliché (eg, billionaire playboy meets ingénue)? If you're writing a war story, has the battle been written about by numerous people before you? If you're writing a popular science book, has someone else covered 'your' topic recently? There's little point writing a book that echoes a title that already exists (or runs counter to all evidence on a topic), unless you're certain you can add something new.

Consider style as well as content. When *Bridget Jones's Diary* came out, the diary format was a fresh approach. A glut of copycat novels when it shot up the charts mean that taking a similar approach now would be seen as dated. Suspense novels and unreliable narrators (eg, *Gone Girl*) have become particularly popular over recent years, but things that are fashionable can soon become unfashionable, so stay on top of the trends to reduce the chances of being perceived as a copycat or rejected for being out of date.

Is Anyone Interested in Your Topic?

For a book to sell, it needs readers. If you're a celebrity, or have a large internet following, this is easier, which is one of the reasons publishers are often biased towards celebrities and/or 'influencers'. If you're not, you need to establish how large an audience there is for your book.

In addition to searching Amazon for similar titles, search social media and Google for websites and communities about your subject or genre. While the occasional author creates their own genre (Chuck Tingle's dinosaur erotica springs to mind), it's easier to get an audience if your book has an established audience base.

Assuming your topic is popular, who are the best sellers and what are the latest book releases? Are there any themes that are particularly common? Look at future releases too. It can take 18 months or more for your book to get published – though sometimes it only takes a few months from getting signed by a publisher, particularly if a book is topical. However, it's best to assume that your book won't come out for at least a year after you've secured a deal, so it's good to get an idea of what the future holds in publishing. Trade publications can be a useful source of information, as they report deals that are being made, not just current releases.

If you self-publish, you can get your book out faster, but it's still worth factoring in time for editing, cover design and marketing: writing your book is just the beginning. And you'll need an even greater awareness of the audience if you self-publish as all the marketing will be down to you (unless you hire someone, which can be costly).

Don't make your job harder than it needs to be by skipping audience research. You don't have to get bogged down in it – some judicious social media 'following' and a few evenings looking through charts should give you a broad idea of the market.

What's Popular?

As you assess what's out there, make a note of styles and themes that are particularly popular. That's not to say you should copy what's out there – not least because publishing has trends and it's often better to create a trend than follow one – but it will give you an idea of what people want to read right now. Are short or long books popular in your genre? Are most of the books in the charts illustrated or plain text? What style of book titles is grabbing people's attention?

Again, reading publishing trade press (The Bookseller, Publishers Weekly), or following them on social media, is a good way to stay ahead of publishing trends and ensure you're not writing a book that will be 'out of fashion' before it's finished. Check international publishing press: if you secure a publishing deal, your book could be sold worldwide so it's worth being aware of overseas markets, not just local ones.

Check the book designs and descriptions too. A strong cover and marketing copy can make a huge difference to sales. Reading the best-seller blurbs will give you an idea of the most effective approach; and noting the most popular cover colours and themes will also guide you when it comes to commissioning or creating your own cover.

Can Your Book Stand Out?

If your book has a niche audience, that's not to say it shouldn't be written. However, the smaller the audience, the less likely you are to attract a publisher. On the plus side, you may become the 'go to' expert in your field, if you bring a subject into the spotlight by writing a brilliant book and publicising it widely.

Conversely, if there's a large potential audience for your book, think about what will make it stand out – and get to know the 'key players' who could help you spread the word, from journalists to social media 'influencers'.

Social media is a good way to grow your personal audience beyond friends and family, ahead of publishing your book. You can use it to connect with others who are interested in your subject and people who are researching or writing about the same subject, who could be potential readers for your book. It's far better to get to know people who can help you market your book before you've written it, so that you can build a genuine relationship with people, than to suddenly 'connect' with your potential audience only when you're trying to sell your book. I'll cover social media in more detail in the marketing chapter.

When Will You Write Your Book?

Next, plan your timing. There's no point setting unrealistic goals: it's often the reason that people end up with part-written books. Instead, work out how much time you have to spend on your book each day or week, and how many words you think you can write in that time. Be honest with yourself. It's better to have a minimum limit that's achievable even when life is busy, than one that's too ambitious.

Next, decide how long your book is going to be. As a rough guide, a short eBook is 5,000-16,000 words, a gift-format book (with pictures) is around 20,000 words, non-fiction is 50,000-80,000 words and a novel is around

80,000 words. Children's books are shorter, depending on the age you're targeting. There's more flexibility with eBooks, and different publishers may have their own word counts for specific series, but it's unlikely you'll get a lot of offers for a 250,000 word epic. If you really feel you need all those words, turn it into a trilogy instead! (Bear in mind there's an equal chance you could be in need of a rigorous editor.)

Once you have your daily and total word counts, you can calculate an 'end date' to work towards. Having a deadline can provide impetus to write; and making it achievable will ensure that writing your book is a pleasure rather than a stressful experience.

The Right Time

I'll outline writing plans in more detail later in the book. However, when planning your time, I'd recommend allowing days off (this goes more so if you're chronically ill or disabled: pacing is essential). Forcing yourself to write daily can make it seem like a chore. Having a weekend or equivalent off, and factoring in time off for birthdays and other key events, will help keep your writing schedule manageable and make it more likely you'll meet your deadline. That's not to say that you can't write on days you haven't scheduled, but these extra days can be used to balance any writing days you have when you're finding it hard to get into the flow.

If your book is topical you'll need to write it quickly: there's no point writing a brilliant book about a topic that has fallen off the news agenda, unless you can add something new to the story. Similarly, if your book is themed around a particular season or event – e.g., Christmas – it is likely to attract seasonal sales, stopping after the festive season has passed. This means you need to get it out well ahead of Christmas to ensure maximum sales. However, anything that limits sales will put publishers off, and reduce your revenue if self-publishing. Consider whether there's any way you can write your book to give it year-round appeal.

If there's no urgency to getting your book out, you can set your own pace. Don't feel obliged to rush. Allowing time to research, mull ideas and let stories develop can help you create a more engaging book – as can having plenty of time for editing. However, it's still worth setting yourself a deadline to work towards, even if it's years away. Just 100 words per day can become a book given enough time*.

In Summary

- Find out what's out there and whether there's an audience for your book before you start writing.
- Decide the best format and length for the book you're going to write.
- Work out how much time you have to write your book
- Give yourself a deadline.

Once you understand your audience and how your book will connect with them, it's time to move to stage two – structuring. Again, this needn't take long, but increases your chances of writing a coherent and readable book.

* A Rabble of Drabbles and Doodles was a book that did just that, written by a disabled author at 100 words per day typed on their phone, collaborating with numerous artists many of whom were also chronically ill, and self-published. It's subsequently raised enough money to buy one person a power wheelchair and provide another person with essential respite care support after their child had a kidney transplant. Self-publishing can sometimes be the easiest way to publish a fundraising book, and there are many ways to define a 'successful' book...

Structuring

Whether you're writing fiction or non-fiction, structuring your book will make it much easier for you to write. It also gives an outline which can come in useful when pitching your book to publishers. While there are numerous guides that help you break your book down into individual scenes and create sophisticated outlines using Post-It notes, you don't need to have a complex structure to write a book. Some people find it easier, but it's entirely possible to write a book from a few key bullet points per chapter (or without any notes at all).

However, having at least some idea of the way your book will unfold will help you avoid getting carried away with excessively long description in one section while skimming details in another. It can help you avoid over-writing, and realising you only have 1,000 words left to bring three major plot points or arguments together, without going over word-count. It can also add confidence to your writing – you know where you're going, even if you're not quite sure how you're going to get there yet...

Summarise your Story

I like to start by writing a single sentence description of the book: an 'elevator pitch'. Pare it back to the core story or argument rather than including all the twists and turns – I aim for a six word summary. For example, *Write Now!* has the core aim of, 'Simplifying writing and promoting a book'.

Write down this sentence and keep it on your desk as a reminder while you're writing. Everything you write should help support or develop your key message. Check as you're going along to avoid veering too far from your aims.

Outline Your Chapters

Now, write your chapter headings. With a non-fiction book, think of the major subjects you need to cover: I tend to opt for 6-10 chapters, though book length dictates it to a degree. The key is to make the book easy for the reader to navigate.

Add a few bullet points under each chapter heading explaining what will be included in your chapter. Is there anything major missing? If so, you may want to add another chapter or two to cover it. Don't worry if some chapters look thinner than others at this point. While you'll want them to be roughly even by the time you finish writing, the structuring stage cab help flag up areas that need more research, or could be combined, or cut.

Try to give your structure a logical flow. Is there basic information that will be required to understand subsequent chapters? Is there a natural chronology? What's your start point and end point?

Keep returning to the core message of your book. How does each chapter reflect this? Writing a book means building a story, even when you're writing non-fiction. Suck your reader in, build your argument or narrative, give them dramatic peaks and leave them with a clear understanding of your message.

Structure Your Story

Entire books have been written about narrative structure. There are academic papers outlining different approaches, and it's well worth spending some time on Google Scholar exploring different views. However, one of the most commonly used is the Mythic Structure, created by Joseph Campbell.

While not without its critics (including me), the Mythic Structure is a classic way to structure fiction. It was famously used by George Lucas when writing Star Wars, among many creatives, and offers a simple framework for a book.

Inspired by Campbell, *The Writer's Journey: Mythic Structure for Writers* by Christopher Vogler, breaks the 'Hero's Journey' down into 12 steps.

- The Ordinary World(The protagonist is introduced in their 'ordinary world')
- Call to Adventure (The protagonist is invited to change the ordinary world)
- Rejection of the Call (They remain in the ordinary world)
- Meeting a Mentor (An influential figure is introduced)
- Crossing the First Threshold (The protagonist takes first steps towards change)
- Tests, Allies and Enemies (Japes ensue)
- Approach to the Innermost Cave (The protagonist almost achieves their dream)
- The Ordeal (The protagonist faces a further trial)
- Reward (The goal is achieved)
- The Road Back (More japes ensue, as loose ends are tied up)
- The Resurrection (True understanding is achieved)
- Return With the Elixir (The protagonist returns to a changed world, and/or as a changed person)

These stages are thought to reflect the human condition: birth, growth, struggle, 'success', wisdom and the death of the old (or sometimes, actual death).

The Mythic Structure gives a simple story arc to follow, though it's also worth Googling The Heroine's Journey for a different perspective on the narrative arc. There are other alternative structures too, so it's worth checking online to discover whether any appeal to you more than the Mythic Structure.

In addition to providing a useful skeleton for your book, having a structure can be useful when a book feels 'messy' during editing. If something feels like it's in the wrong place, check whether it would fit elsewhere in your chosen structure more effectively. Sometimes, all the words are there but they're in the wrong place. However, structuring your book, however loosely, before you start can help minimise this risk.

The Benefits of Structure

Applying an established structure to your chapter outline will help you check the order is logical, and designed for maximum dramatic impact. If you're writing a book with the intention of providing it in serial format, each chapter should also echo your overall structure, to urge the reader to buy the next chapter. However, don't feel you have to be rigid when following a specific narrative structure. It's not an essential part of the process but it can provide a useful guide to pacing your book in the most engaging way, and help you work out which scenes should take place in which points of the book.

Some people find that a structure confines them, resulting in formulaic writing. If you don't feel that your writing can flow, loosen up your structure. Alternatively, you could plot your novel along the mythic structure and then choose to subvert it.

The act of writing a book often changes the way a story will grow. Characters may develop in ways that you don't expect, new plot points may emerge and whole new stories may be uncovered. Stephen King describes writing as 'archaeology', with the writer letting a story reveal itself. Having too rigid a structure may mean that you miss the subtler stories.

Maintain Balance

The trick is to have enough of a structure to know where the story is going and enough imagination to be prepared to deviate from the route should something more appealing emerge. A sound structure can be a good way to motivate yourself as you write, helping you order your thoughts. It can also mean that you can write the book in the order that you want to rather than starting on the first page and finishing at 'The End', if you wish. A bad structure can keep you so bogged down in detail that the book feels plodding and wooden, and you never get into 'the flow'.

Make sure you don't use structuring your book as an excuse to procrastinate. While you can use a solid structure to help sell your book to agents and publishers, you'll still need to write your book in order to get a deal – and unless you're an established author or a celebrity, you'll almost certainly have to show your completed book to have any hope of attracting attention. However, once you've got your structure in place, it should help speed your writing.

In Summary

- Summarise your book in a sentence.
- Write a chapter outline.
- Add a few bullet points per chapter.
- Check the narrative has peaks and troughs at appropriate places to maintain momentum.
- Identify any weak points.

Once you have an idea of structure, it's easier to see the gaps in your knowledge or plot. The next step is filling these gaps with research.

Researching

You may already have stacks of research. You might be starting from scratch. If it's the former, gather your research together and divide it into chapters. This helps make it manageable as you can read all the research for your first chapter, write the chapter, then move on to reading the research for your second chapter. It also means you're less likely to forget it.

If you're thin on research for any chapter, make a note in your chapter outline. Research is a great way to spend time if writing isn't flowing – and can often spark ideas to break through 'writers' block' too. Having a list of the research you need to do can make it easier for you to fill specific gaps you need to, rather than having the whole of the internet to distract you.

Even if you're writing fiction, there could be research to do. If your character travels anywhere, you'll need to know how long it takes. If they work in a low-paid job, are they living in an area where that's feasible? If you mention a real location, have you got the geography of the area spot on? Inauthenticity can be a major turn-off for the reader. That doesn't mean you can't let your writing flow, but make sure you fact check it once it's written.

Research Tools

The research you do will obviously depend on the book you're writing. I've used tools ranging from Google Maps to Google Scholar, along with reading books, visiting archives, museums and libraries, and talking to experts.

While many writers use Wikipedia as a starting point for research, and it can certainly be a useful tool, make sure you refer to primary sources too. Not only will this give you a fuller picture, but it can also spark new ideas: primary sources often contain a lot more nuance than bare quotes or abstracts alone.

If you're writing a historical novel, can you find letters from the time, to give you an idea of the way in which people really communicated? If you're writing about a real person, seeing their handwriting, family tree or even a list of their expenses can provide extra inspiration and insight into the person you're writing about. Better yet, can you talk to someone who was alive at the time, or knew people or events you are writing about? Interviewing people face to face is one option, along with email interviews and phone conversations.

Visiting libraries and museums can also help you get a feel for time or place, and can be particularly useful when writing historical novels. Pay attention to the way a place smells as well as the way it looks and the sounds you can hear. By engaging all your senses with places you're researching, you're more likely to notice tiny details that can inform your book.

Research is Everywhere

Don't just see research as books, academic papers, historical sources or interviews with people. Some research is as simple as noting down wording of public announcements or paying attention to someone chatting to a friend on the bus and noting the way they communicate (and how long it takes the bus to get to its destination). If you're writing fiction, every encounter offers a potential character: strangers' conversations can be useful inspiration. You can take notes in your phone or carry a notebook for any observations. It can also be useful to record conversations if you find it hard to write dialogue. However, this is a request that's best kept for friends and formal interviewees: don't record people without their permission!

'Write what you know,' is such standard advice as to be a cliché. It doesn't mean you need to write an autobiography – unless you've had a particularly fascinating life (and other people agree!). However, you can draw on memories and experiences to add colour to your work. It can help you avoid clichés too. For example, focus on your body when you're in an emotional state from joy to anger. Think about where you're feeling the emotion, and exactly what the sensation is like to avoid hackneyed 'curdling stomachs' or 'racing hearts'. Watch others when they're emotional to see where they are tense. Not all research draws on the written word.

Some books are more research heavy than others. That doesn't mean you should delay writing. However, you may want to allow more time for content to 'simmer' if you have a lot of research to digest. I tend to start by broadly researching the area I want to write about, identifying the angle I want to take, writing a loose outline and filling in missing research as the book evolves. There are times when I'll get stuck and need to take a research break, but I'll often start writing a book knowing that there are key texts I need to read before I can complete the book.

This is one of the reasons that it can be a joy to self publish. If you only have your own deadlines to work to, you can spend however much time a book takes to ensure it's polished. You may write your first draft, only to realise that you want to take a totally different direction now the book's finished. You may discover research that renders your core idea nonsensical. This is why it's important to get the balance right between research and procrastination.

By self-publishing, you can take all the time you need to develop your book, without having someone else's deadline to work to. If you're new to writing, this can relieve pressure – though don't become so complacent about deadlines that you never get round to publishing it...

All Sources Are Not Created Equal

If you're writing non-fiction, you need to ensure your research is rigorous for it to be taken seriously (this is a topic covered brilliantly in The Research Companion by Dr Petra Boynton, particularly if you're writing an academic book).

While you may want to present a particular argument, your book will be far better if you acknowledge any conflicting sources and develop your ideas around existing evidence, even if you present a new or challenging approach.

With fiction, if a character's citing a fact, it doesn't have to be true – after all, people get things wrong. However, this should be used as a personality trait of your character, not an excuse for sloppy research.

Don't get so intimidated by research that you give up on writing. It may be that you've already internalised a lot of what you want to say, and can start writing, filling any gaps with research at a later date. If you feel like you're spending too much time on research, and not enough on writing, you probably are.

Organising Your Research

You can save yourself hours of research by organizing it as you complete it. If you're writing about a person (whether fictional or real), make a timeline of key events, to help you ensure your chronology is in place. You can use a calendar (for the year your book is set in) to help with this, or simply create an ordered list.

Similarly, add quotes and citations to a list by chapter. That way, you can simply copy and paste them as required. This process will also help you spot any repetition, and decide where best each piece of material fits in your book.

Sort any physical resources such as letters or notes into order too. You can speed the writing process by having everything you need to hand, to refer to at a glance.

With fiction, you may find character 'cheat sheets' save you time. These include details such as eye colour, birthday and any other key 'minor' information that you may need to ensure your character is consistent throughout the book. Some people write elaborate character outlines, including everything from their character's favourite food to their childhood hobbies. Others keep it simpler. You can choose whichever approach works best for you – or skip character cheat sheets altogether. However, I find they save time when writing fiction for anything longer than a short story.

In Summary

- Gather together all the research in chapter order.
- Read through it to refresh your memory, noting down any key points you want to cover.
- Slot any new key points into your structure.
- List any gaps in research that will need filling as you go along.
- Read chapter one research.
- Prepare to Write Now!

Writing

Writing a book is a marathon, not a sprint (though you can start with a 10km jog by opting to write a short book to start with). This means pacing is all important. Rather than setting aside ambitious writing days when you plan to write 10,000 words in a day, make writing manageable around your everyday life. Little and often is better than big but rare.

If you have days when you can't write, don't give up. Use the time for research instead. If you've made notes of queries as you go along, and written down any research gaps, you have a ready-made list of things to discover. I often find that research energises or inspires me, and leads me back to writing.

If not, researching assuages writer's guilt, which can often hamper writing. Keeping yourself feeling confident that you're on track can help you avoid 'the fear' setting in. It also means that you've got the facts you need ready to slot into your book – which all adds to the word count.

Setting the Word Count

'How many words do you write in a day?' is a common question from new writers. It's almost impossible to answer as it depends on the kind of writing you're doing. Some writing requires understanding and simplifying complex research. Some requires intense creativity. It also depends on the individual, and what else is going on in their life. The more you write, the faster you're likely to be, but everyone has ebbs and flows.

I like to divide word counts into 500 word chunks, as that's an amount I can easily fit into most days, regardless of what other work I have on. If I'm focused on a project, that could increase to 2,500 per day, and I've had deadlines requiring 5,000+ words in a day. I've seen many writers say that 1,000 words per day is a comfortable amount. However, even 100 words per day results in a short ebook in 50 days, so pick an amount that seems manageable to you. You can always increase it if you find yourself writing more than you expected.

As a rough guide, writing 500 words per day equates to a novel in eight months. Writing 1,000 words per day brings that down to four months, and if you want to write a novel in a month, you'll need to write around 2,700 words per day. It adds up even faster if you're writing a shorter book: a 16,000 word ebook can take you a month or less, even with relatively low daily word counts.

Maintaining Momentum

Some writers prefer to work to a tighter deadline, with more pressure on. National Novel Writing Month, popularly known as NaNoWriMo, takes place each November and attracts a huge number of writers who commit to producing 50,000 words in a month. Some find this helps them put together the skeleton of a full length novel. However, their attitude to AI has put a lot of people off, as have various other issues over recent years, so you may want to read up on it before deciding whether you want to join in.

There are also numerous writing communities that you can join online, whether on Facebook, BlueSky or as websites in their own right. Writing virtually alongside other people can offer a sense of community, which may appeal to writers who feel lonely working without anyone else to talk to. People who find it hard to commit to a deadline may find the shared commitment provides extra motivation to keep on writing.

However, unless you thrive under tight deadlines, there's no need to write your book at speed. Let it take the time it needs to. Having time to consider your book as you're writing it may help you develop it further. New ideas may emerge as you uncover new research, and you may need time to mull over ideas, no matter how much you've planned in advance. If you get a subsequent publishing deal, you'll be working to someone else's deadline. Writing your first book gives you the luxury of all the time you need. The only deadline is the one you set yourself.

If you've never written a book before, you may want to start with a short one. That way, you can learn the publishing process without having to deal with 80,000 words worth of writing and editing. It can also help you build your audience – and build your confidence before tackling a longer book.

Avoiding Writer's Block

If you're a professional writer, writer's block is not an option, unless you have an independent source of income. Writers write – even if the words that emerge are far from beautiful. However, every writer will have moments when writing is tough. I tend to spend time researching if I'm finding writing a struggle. It occupies my time in a useful way, and I often find that it inspires new ideas.

If you're struggling with a particular section of your book, you can try moving to a different part to see if that flows more easily. There's no rule saying a book has to be written in order. If you're in a bad mood, write a part of the book that could use your ire. If you're feeling philosophical, tackle a more thoughtful part of your book. This is where your structure comes in handy, as it helps keep your book on track even when you're jumping between sections.

You can also try re-reading your book. While it's easy to get bogged down by re-reading your book every time you start writing – something that is sure to make you bored of your opening chapter – if you use times when you're struggling with writing to edit your book instead, it's still taking it one step closer to being published.

Avoiding Anxiety

Getting anxious about writing is one of the easiest ways to help writer's block thrive. If you feel yourself getting so caught up in worrying about writing that you stop writing, take a break. Go for a walk. Some of the most famous writers swore by the power of nature, and taking time to look at the clouds or feed the birds can help you relax, and take your mind off writing. Once you've had a refreshing break away from the blank page, you may well find the words flow much more easily.

Don't make the mistake of 'waiting for the muse to strike'. You don't need to be in the mood to write in order to finish your book. Just keep typing one word after another. You can always edit it at a later date if a section feels wooden or out of place.

Some people swear by writing prompts or creative exercises. I've never found them particularly useful, but if you do, try one of these.

- Write about the last time you experienced joy.
- Write about your character's earliest memory.
- Write a description of something on your desk.
- Write about something you can smell right now.
- Describe yourself in 50 words (this can come in handy if you get booked for any literary events too).

You could have a bath, chat to a friend or do anything else that distracts yourself from worrying. Unless you've already got a publisher, there's no real pressure for you to finish by a set date. If you really can't find any words to write, give yourself a day off. There's always tomorrow.

Editing

Once your book is written, it's time to edit. Ideally, put your book aside for a month, or at least a couple of weeks, before you move on to the editing stage. You need to approach your book as a reader rather than a writer in order to be an effective editor.

However, it's too easy for writers to miss phrases they overuse or concepts that aren't made clear to the reader. This is why it's always best to have a separate editor for your book: a fresh perspective from an expert will result in a better book.

Don't give your book to anyone else to edit until you've been through it thoroughly yourself. Spellcheck your book, and make sure it's as polished as it can be before you ask for comment: it's not fair to expect someone to wade through amends you could easily have made yourself (unless you're paying an editor, in which case it just means more expense for you.)

Dealing With Editors

If you don't have any budget, ask a well-read friend to proof read your book at the very least. Don't ask someone who's likely to tell you it's brilliant for fear of hurting your feelings. Instead, choose the person who corrects your grammar on Facebook posts, or is known for their honesty. Editing is not about ego-inflation: it's about getting a book into the best shape it can possibly be.

Don't argue with your editor over every change. While you don't need to make every change that's recommended, if you trust your editor, that means listening to what they say. This goes doubly if you're asking someone to edit your book for free. They're being kind enough to give you their time. Don't reward them with an earful of insecure outrage when they're doing something to help you. That doesn't mean you have to make every change that's suggested, but avoid getting defensive.

Editing can be a tough process, particularly if you've never shared your work before. You may find sentences that you lovingly crafted are sacrificed because they don't resonate with the reader in the way you'd hoped, or ruin the flow of copy. But a good editor can make your words shine.

In Summary

- Set your word count.
- Set your deadline.
- Research or edit when writing is proving hard.

- Avoid anxiety – and subsequent writer's block - with self-care.
- Edit your book.

Once your book is written and edited, it's time to publish it. You may want to find a publisher, or you could choose to publish it yourself. Whichever option you choose, there's still a bit more work to do before you can get your book into reader's hands.

Publishing

You've now written your book – congratulations! The next step is getting it out into the world. You have two main options: get a publisher to buy your book or publish it yourself. There is a third option, in the form of vanity publishing. However, this can often be a very expensive way of doing things and self-publishing options are generally preferable, particularly now that there are so many online tools to make the process as simple as possible. (There are also hybrid publishers, somewhere between vanity press and self-publishing. Check with their existing authors to see how reputable they are as some hybrid publishers are better than others.)

While it's great that you've finished writing your book, publishers tend to be inundated with books. Very few publishers accept unsolicited manuscripts, so if you want your book published, rather than self-publishing it, you'll need an agent.

Getting an Agent

Getting an agent means pitching yourself. Publishing is about making money so you need to convince your agent that you're a bankable proposition. When pitching your book to an agent, send an outline along with details of your social media following, press contacts and anything else that will help you sell your book. If you have a famous relative who will give you a quote for the cover of your book, now's the time to mention them. If you're speaking at any conferences, going on radio or TV or have other ways you could promote your book, mention it. Agents represent authors based on the whole package, not just the book that they've written.

Don't just send your outline to every agent you can find. The Writers' and Artists' Yearbook is a valuable resource that includes details of agents interests and genres. There's no point sending your brilliantly written fantasy novel to a non-fiction agent, or your romance novel to an agent who specialises in crime thrillers.

Once you've identified a few relevant potential agents, research them online. Find out who else they represent, if they have a manuscript wishlist, and which books they've sold. Follow them on social media to see whether you agree with their approach and style. By finding an agent who's the right fit, you're a lot more likely to succeed. If all goes well, they could be in your life for a long time.

Don't feel disheartened if the first agent turns you down. Publishing is a numbers game from start to finish, and many bestselling authors were rejected multiple times before finally becoming 'overnight' successes. Keep pitching, but do take any comments into consideration. If you're told the same thing by many agents, you may need to make some changes to your book or approach.

Writing an Outline

In the first instance, your agent will use your outline to pitch your book to publishers. As a general outline, summarise the book in a single paragraph, then provide a short chapter breakdown with 2-3 bullet points per chapter (NB: for fiction, you will be more likely to be asked for the first three chapters along with a synopsis, and will be expected to have the completed manuscript ready if the agent likes the synopsis and sample copy).

Add a paragraph about any competitors, along with any information on the size of the market that you have (e.g., Publishing News recently reported an xx% growth in xxx market')

Finally, include a brief biography that shows how saleable a prospect you are. Mention any qualifications you have that make you the best person to write the book, along with any promotional routes at your disposal.

It can be tempting to approach agents ahead of writing your book. However, even with non-fiction, publishers tend to require at least the first 10,000 words, along with your outline, and may well set tight deadlines even if they do buy on a partially completed book, so you'll make your life much easier by finishing your book before approaching agents. It's unlikely an agent will take a new writer on based on nothing more than a short extract and good faith (unless you're a celebrity, in which case you probably don't need this book).

Self-publishing

If you plan on self-publishing, you don't need an agent. However, it's still worth having a brief outline of your book, to use for promotion. You will need 'back cover blurb', which can double as your book description for online listings. Start your promotion well ahead of publication. You can list a book as a pre-release on Amazon, helping build pre-sales and providing you with a sales link for anything you write about the book before it comes out.

Do Judge a Book by Its Cover

When publishing your book, you also need a cover, and it's important you get it right. While Amazon does offer ready-made covers as part of its free Kindle publishing package, these may not suit your aesthetic, and are a lot less likely to stand out than something unique and well designed.

Unless you've worked in cover design, this is a job that's well worth outsourcing to a designer. Search for book cover designers online, and approach any whose work appeals to you. There are many people who make a living out of eBook cover design, and it needn't be prohibitively costly. Do remember the saying, 'If you pay peanuts, you get monkeys' though. The cheapest designer isn't always the best investment long-term (and AI is best avoided as it puts many people off, because it takes designer's jobs. I think creatives should stick together, so would never knowingly choose an AI cover design).

Check book cover design trends and find some covers that you like to give the designer a steer. Check their portfolio for similar work: while designers can obviously adapt their style, if you can find someone with a similar visual aesthetic, it makes briefing them a lot easier.

Self-Publishing Practicalities

While there are alternatives to Amazon, it's by far the biggest book retailer. Amazon is also keen to encourage people to self-publish, and has a selection of free tools to make the process as simple as possible. With a ready-made potential audience, it's the easiest place to start as a self-publisher.

You can sign up with the Kindle Direct Publishing Programme for free, and use it to create books, previewing them before publishing them and even creating print-on-demand paperbacks. Amazon takes a commission based on the price and other features of your book.

You need to format your book for Kindle publication, but this can be done simply using Word. The Kindle Publishing site includes a useful help section to take you through the details, which are no more complex than bolding copy. If your book includes tables or pictures, it can be a little trickier. However, you can create different types of books using the different Amazon templates: pick the right one for your book to make life easier.

Once you've uploaded your book, Amazon provides eBook viewers so you can check that you're happy with the way your book appears before publishing it. Do not skip this step. It's easy for errors to emerge at this stage, and something as simple as a chapter being rendered in 'headline' font could ruin the experience for readers. Make sure you edit your book once it's been turned into an eBook as well as editing it before uploading.

Don't make the mistake of thinking your book will be published as soon as you submit it. All books on Amazon are approved before publication, to ensure that content adheres to Amazon guidelines. This can take anything from a day to a few weeks, so make sure you read the guidelines and allow plenty of time for approval if you have a specific publication date in mind. There's no point releasing a Valentine's book that isn't approved until 15th February. Finally, upload your cover. Make sure it's the right size, to ensure it appears without being pixelated or otherwise cropped.

Pricing Your Book

Look at other books that are available in the market and price your book competitively. Don't think your book needs to be the cheapest one available to sell: you can always reduce the price but putting the price up is unlikely to get a good reaction.

Value your words – but be reasonable too. Pricing a short eBook as you'd price a full-length novel is unlikely to be well-received by readers. Offer value for money and they'll be more likely to come back for more of your books in the future.

Some people produce series of books, with the first at a low price and subsequent books in the series having escalated prices. Amazon also allows you to promote your book by offering it for free, or running a price promotion. Careful use of this can help boost your sales by increasing your visibility in the charts. Amazon includes clear explanations of what you need to do to run a promotion, so you don't need to be a marketing genius to put your promotional campaign together.

Categories and Keywords

When selling your book online, make sure you choose the right category for your book to increase its chance of success. Broad fiction categories will have a lot more chart competition than more tailored ones. If you're not sure which category is right for you, look at bestsellers in the category and see whether your book would be a good fit, and what competition you face in that chart.

A more niche category may have less competition but it may also have less visibility. The trick is to get the balance right between having a reasonable audience and minimal competition from best-selling authors.

Using the right keywords when listing your book on Amazon can also make a big difference. You can find keywords that people commonly search for using online tools, such as Google Adwords Keyword tool. It makes sense to use commonly used keywords, to have the largest potential audience. However, make sure they represent your book accurately.

Don't include your name as a keyword unless you're already a best-selling author. Instead, think of topics that your book covers well, and choose high-ranking keywords that reflect this.

Your back cover blurb should also include some of your keywords to ensure readers know exactly what to expect, and boost search engine results. Use these keywords in blog posts about your book too. Consistent use of the right keywords – without 'keyword stuffing' and making copy unreadable - can be used to lead new readers to your book.

In Summary

- Decide whether you want to approach publishers or self-publish.
- Write an outline of your book.
- Approach agents if you are not self-publishing.
- Get a great cover if self-publishing.
- Format your book if self-publishing.
- Price your book if self-publishing.
- Choose the right categories and keywords if self-publishing.

Now, you're on to the final stage – which is arguably as important as writing the book: promotion. No matter how brilliant your book is, there's no point publishing it if you're not going to promote it. Even if you have a publisher, you'll still be expected to do all you can to help the book sell.

Effective promotion can make all the difference between a book that is published and a book that is widely read.

Promoting

Nowadays, promotion is an essential part of a writer's role. While publishers will provide books with marketing support, they tend to have small publicity teams promoting multiple authors. This means that, even if you get a publishing deal, you'll need to do the bulk of the marketing yourself.

Social Media

Marketing takes many forms. Many publishers look to social media statistics to see whether an author is worth investing in. Having a strong social media following, or a popular author's page on Facebook will make your book more appealing.

Be warned: social media can also be a huge time sap. It's easy to procrastinate, convincing yourself that you're doing something useful when your 'admiring kitten pictures' to work ratio suggests otherwise. Scheduling social media can be a good way to reduce the amount of time that you waste, although it does need to be balanced with 'live' posts and authentic responses to help you develop a connection with your audience (and potential readers).

Scheduling Posts

There are various free services available to schedule posts, depending on which social media channels you use (paid for upgrades are available but it's unlikely you'll need these unless you're managing multiple social media accounts). You can also schedule posts in Facebook, using the 'Publishing Tools' tab. This means that you can send out daily social media posts without having to go online every day (though it's worth checking in on a regular basis to make sure you respond promptly to any questions.)

Don't just post self-promotional messages. Give people a reason to follow you. And don't post anything online that you wouldn't say in person – and don't mind sharing with the world. You could post links to stories that inspire you, writing tips you find useful or research around the topic of your book. Posts with images attract a lot more social media interest than ones that are text only. Make sure you include Alt Text so that people using screen readers can access the image, and you don't lose out on potential readers: an increasing amount of people refuse to share images without Alt Text so you're unnecessarily losing audience and making your promotion less accessible. Video is even more engaging, and live video formats also tend to attract more people. Make sure you include captions and ideally, don't rely on auto-captioning – the captions generated are known as 'craptions' for a reason, and often don't reflect what's being said. Inclusivity aside, don't be too formulaic about what you post: the idea is to build a genuine audience of people who enjoy the content that you share.

Facebook

While Facebook makes it increasingly hard to promote posts without spending money, you can still use it to drive book sales. You can share links on your personal profile or create a page for the book. Include lots of visuals, from memes to your book cover, as visual posts tend to achieve much higher engagement than text-based ones.

You can also create a 'Facebook party' to have an online book launch. To do this, create an event page and invite others to join you in celebrating your book launch online at a set time (making sure to include the time-zone). The Facebook party could involve book giveaways or sharing extracts, and celebrate a single book or a number of author's new releases (for example, tying in with Disability History Month, or finding a common bond between writers, such as nature, being debut writers, or all being over a certain age. The latter approach can help increase the audience, offering a great way for authors to collaborate to mutual benefit.

Facebook Live is another visual way to let people know about your book, whether as part of a Facebook party or as a stand-alone piece of marketing. Don't think you have to be a polished TV professional: 'authentic' videos tend to be more popular. Be yourself and let your passion for your book shine through.

Creating a solid BlueSky following (as many writers have moved from Twitter) may drive book sales – initial reports seem positive. In addition to sharing other people's books, and engaging with their skeets, to develop and grow your audience, you can drive book sales through hosting a book-themed chat on the day of launch. If your book is an anthology, you could also create a Starter Pack or feed of all the contributing writers.

A book-themed chat involves using a themed hashtag to talk about a specific topic. Run a virtual #BookLaunch by inviting people to join you for a chance to read extracts and maybe win prizes on the day that your book launches by following and sharing your hashtag. Keep your launch relatively brief to ensure followers don't feel overwhelmed by messages – ideally, around an hour. Promote your book launch for a few weeks beforehand so that people know what to expect and can put a date in their diary. Make sure there's enough incentive for them to get involved: no one just wants to hear an hour of 'Buy my book'.

You can increase engagement by asking guests to answer certain questions – for example, 'Which fairytale character would you invite to a party?' or 'Which author do you find the most inspiring?' This will spark more conversation than simply offering a discount on your book. Tailor your questions to the audience and book, of course: the former question is unlikely to sell many war memoirs or thrillers

When people answer, comment on their responses. The closer a connection you can form with people, the more likely they are to buy your book. That doesn't mean faking friendliness with everyone, and developing parasocial relationships, but be genuine and polite when people comment. Support other writers and they'll be more likely to support you.

Hashtag Hours

You can also drive traffic to your book using hashtag hours. These are themed around specific places or topics, such as #MigraineHour or #GardenChat. Search for hashtag hours that are relevant to your book, and follow the tag for a while without commenting, to get an idea of the best approach. Some hashtag hours are purely promotional. Others actively seek to reduce self-promotion, and you don't want to spam a hashtag.

However, letting people in your area know that you have a book out, or sharing links to it from a book promotional tag can be an easy way to expand your audience. Do help other people on the hashtag too, by sharing anything you like. You're more likely to have your content shared if you share other people's relevant content.

Don't think that you have to post huge amounts of 'content'. While you will attract more interest by posting more frequently, endless pleas that people buy your book are unlikely to reap rewards. If you don't have something that's worth sharing, don't post anything.

As a rough guide, one promotional post to seven 'interesting' ones should keep your social media followers engaged without making your social media feed feel dull and repetitive. Don't feel that you can only share interesting links once though, particularly on BlueSky. If you've written a blog post, feel free to link to it several times. Try changing the description you use to see if it attracts more attention. Track how many likes and shares your post generates to work out the most effective approach.

Some social media channels offer free analytics. If so, make sure you check them. And if you have a website, enabling Google analytics will help you see where your traffic is coming from, and how many people click through to your sales page, if you have one.

Blogging and Newsletters

Creating your own blog or newsletter is also worth considering. This gives you a chance to develop a fan-base for your writing, and give people an idea of what to expect from your book. Don't just fill it with extracts from your book: if too much is available for free online, people won't bother buying it (and it won't be eligible for the Kindle Unlimited scheme which could limit your audience.)

Instead, use your blog or newsletter to build your profile. You might write about research trips you've been on for your book. You could share writing tips, or simply develop an online presence that represents who you are (however accurately – if you're writing under a pseudonym, 'public' you may be very different from the real thing). You could include links to other writing you've done, or other writers you rate. Your blog or newsletter is as unique as your book, but should be considered as a potential marketing tool. It can also be a good way to maintain a regular writing habit when you're 'between books', which can make writing the next book easier.

Email marketing has become more complex as new data protection regulations have come in. If you want to create a mailing list, only add people who've asked to be added to your list, and make it easy for people to opt out. Many people use MailChimp for this, which automates a lot of the process, making life easier. Wordpress also has newsletter functionality, for a fee.

However you put your newsletter together, don't send hundreds of emails. Make sure that any email you send has something that benefits the reader, from a link to a free book extract to a competition or discount voucher, rather than flooding them with messages to buy your book. You could also include books by other authors that you think your newsletter readers may enjoy: share the love.

Press

Traditional press can make a difference to book sales too, particularly if the publication has a large audience and syndicates stories (or if you can get on TV). One piece of coverage about your book can get worldwide exposure. However, you're only likely to attract press coverage if you have a good story and a strong hook.

Remember that magazines tend to work around three months ahead so if you're pitching a Valentine's Day book, you'll need to send information out in November. Newspapers obviously have shorter lead times but unless your book is news-based, it's still worth pitching them ahead of release, in case there are any larger features you could fit into.

Make sure you pitch your book to the right person. Sending press releases to the editor is unlikely to work unless it's a very small title. The Books Editor or Arts Editor is the obvious choice if the publication has one. If you're pitching a feature-led angle, pitch the Features Editor, unless there's a particular journalist you think would be interested in your book.

Research the journalists who write about your topic. Better yet, do you know any journalists? If not, you can find journalists and editors on social media, but you're unlikely to get a positive response if you just spam people with messages about your book. Instead, follow target journalists, see what they're interested in, connect with them over common interests, help out with any #JournoRequests they may have and you'll be a lot more likely to get a positive response when you mention your book.

Are there any magazines or newspapers that would be interested in your book? What is it that makes your book worth writing about? Is there any news hook that makes your book more topical? Can you persuade anyone to review your book? Interviews are another option but unless you're famous, you're unlikely to secure an interview without a strong story.

Local Media

For local press and radio, you can try 'Local author writes book' but you're likely to need a more engaging hook to secure interest. Could you give a talk on writing at your local library to give a news hook? Was your book inspired by anything or anyone based locally? Is there a 'hearts and minds' story behind your book, with a local angle?

Don't be surprised if you do a radio interview only to realise the presenter hasn't read your book (and do re-read your book prior to radio interviews. These can often happen many months after you wrote the book and you don't want to get tripped up by being asked about something you've only got a dim recollection of writing.)

National Press

If the story is strong enough, you can approach national press. If you're donating a percentage of your book's profits to charity, this could give a hook. Again, a 'hearts and minds' story may work but you'll need to make sure it's original, and that you've got lots of photographs you're willing to share. 'Author Writes Book After Illness', or 'Author Recovers From Break Up by Writing Book' are unlikely to be unique enough to attract national interest.

While you need to have confidence in your book, don't assume that journalists will share your enthusiasm. Playing the diva in interviews is unlikely to attract a positive write-up. Instead, try to be succinct, and give the journalist interesting stories to work with. The more compelling a story you can create, the more space you're likely to get in a publication.

Creating a Chart-Topping Campaign

Regardless of the methods you use, all promotion should drive book sales to help you get into the charts – and pre-sales are an essential way to build interest, as all pre-sales count in the first week of your book's release so the more copies you pre-sell, the greater your chance of charting, and thus getting greater visibility for your book.

Pre-sales aside, try to time your activity so that it's all focused around a set date – and follow your stats on Amazon closely all day. It's much easier to chart if you're selling several copies of a book in an hour rather than spread across a week. Designing your promotions in the right way will help you increase your chances of getting a chart position – ready to screen-grab and use in subsequent promotion, if you do end up charting.

It's much easier to get into an Amazon sub-genre chart than the overall bestseller lists, but getting this visibility is a great way to drive further sales. There are millions of books on Amazon, and being in the charts means that people who are browsing for ideas are more likely to see yours, and view it positively. Charting also gives you a promotional angle to use to drive future book sales. Focusing activity around a specific date will boost your chances of charting. Get publicity out there well ahead of launch date but focus advertising and other promotional activity around your launch date.

Book Extracts

Book extracts can form a central part of your marketing strategy: use the words you've already written. If someone likes a book extract, they're more likely to enjoy the book. However, don't share so much of your book that it's not worth someone buying it. Instead, choose two or three extracts of 500-800 words that reflect well on the book, and work on a stand-alone basis.

For a non-fiction title, you can turn it into an article – e.g., if your book is about gardening, your extract may be about how to plant tomatoes. For a fiction title, pick extracts that suck the reader into the action and entice them to read more. You can include a single line to introduce context at the top of your extract, but it's better if it works on an entirely stand-alone basis.

You can share book extracts through exchanging guest posts with other bloggers, if you have a blog, or uploading them to sites such as Medium and Huffington Post. You can also use your extracts across social media.

You may choose to make a video or audio recording of your extract – for example, making a recording of you reading at a local library or book shop. If you do, make sure you include captions and a transcript for accessibility.

Launch Parties

Even if you have a major publisher, it's unlikely there will be marketing budget set aside for a launch party. However, if you know lots of journalists, or just want to celebrate your book's launch, it needn't be complicated to put together.

Many bars will give you an area for free, particularly on quiet nights of the week, and you may be able to provide a free drink from a sponsor if you ask nicely, assuming you can find a drink brand that the venue stocks. You can also look at alternative spaces. I used a shop for one launch, providing a cheese board and bread for people to snack on, along with wine. Cheese turned out to be a remarkably popular choice, and it was much cheaper and easier than canapes (after making 300 crostini for a launch party many years ago, I strongly recommend cheese, including vegan options. Life's too short to mass-cater unless that's in your skill set. (Obviously, if you've written a cookery book, making the food yourself makes sense.)

If you can't find a bar for free, or don't want to be around alcohol, consider quirkier options: a picnic in a park, a launch party on a beach, or try chatting to your local library to see if they would be happy for you to host your launch party there. Whichever option you go for, take a pile of books, invite anyone you know who might be interested and include local press on your list, along with any local literary event organisers and library staff. You can sell books at your launch to help cover the cost, or simply invite friends to a celebratory drink in a bar on the day your book launches, so it doesn't cost you anything at all. Better yet, go for an online launch party as that makes it accessible to more people – and you can record it to have a memory of the event.

Unless you have high profile friends or it's a particularly impressive party, it's unlikely you'll generate much press from a launch party. You may sell a few books but you'd (possibly) be surprised how many people will ask you for a free book. However, a launch party gives an opportunity for you to get photographs of people with your book for social media, as well as allowing you to connect with people directly, and maybe give a reading from the book, which could be recorded for use on social media. That said, you don't have to have a launch party for your book at all: very few authors do nowadays and it's unlikely to have a huge effect on marketing or sales.

Reviews

Reviews are a key way to drive sales. You can't just ask friends to review your book on Amazon (unless they've bought it online). However, you can incentivise it. For example, Amazon allows you to provide your book for free, for five days in every ninety. If you choose to use this function, ask people to review your book when promoting the free offer. It won't guarantee reviews but some kind people are likely to do as you ask.

You can also offer book bloggers free copies of your book in exchange for reviews. This can be a great way to build grass-roots support for a book, assuming the bloggers like it.   Reviewing books on your own blog can be another way to encourage others to review your books: some authors will happily trade reviews.

There are people offering paid reviewed services. However, these are often spam engines and it's best to keep to legitimate methods to generate reviews. Sending out press copies to websites and publications you think will enjoy it is a legitimate way to get reviews (though it's always best to include the book as a download link rather than a document, rather than emailing huge files). Buying reviews is unlikely to generate authentic results.

Make Life Easy on Yourself

If all this seems like a lot of hard work and a lot to learn, don't worry. Luckily, The Empowered Author exists. Created by Katie Sadler and Sam

Missingham, both award-winning book marketers who've worked with many of the UK's bestselling and well-respected authors, it has free resources galore, and really reasonable support services from online workshops to one-to-one marketing advice and support.

Sam was Head of Audience Development at HarperCollins where she was responsible for running large marketing campaigns across their entire book list. Before this, she was Head of Events & Marketing at The Bookseller magazine where she ran the industry awards, conferences, subscriptions and launched the FutureBook community. Katie Sadler started working with Sam on The Empowered Author in 2021, and runs the 2000+ strong Facebook group where The Empowered Author encourage and support authors of every background to make better marketing choices. Katie started working in publishing in 2007, going from Ebury Publishing to HarperCollins fiction and then Quercus Books. Since becoming self-employed, she's worked with all three companies again, as well as Orion Books, Little, Brown, numerous independent publishers and directly with authors, to help them create sustainable marketing plans that get results.

Between Sam and Katie, there's not a lot they don't know. Whether you need a crash course on Booktok, inspiration for creating a pre-sales campaign or someone to hold your hand through the whole process of marketing your book, they have something useful on offer – and loads of free resources. Sign up to their newsletter for to keep up to date with publishing trends and the best ways to promote your book – it's free. They also offer a free Creative Archive – "the only database of book marketing creative assets - trailers, ads, cover reveals, unboxing videos, social, print and more across all genres." to help inspire your own marketing. Marketing moves fast, particularly when it comes to social media, but if you use The Empowered Author, you can stay up to date with what matters.

In Summary

- Establish a presence on social media.
- Create your own blog.
- Connect with journalists and influencers.
- Create a compelling story for media.
- Plan a launch campaign for a specific day.
- Generate reviews
- Sign up to TheEmpoweredAuthor.com newsletter

Conclusion

There are millions of books published each year. If your first book doesn't top the charts, get you fan mail from adoring readers or bring you record returns, don't feel too disheartened. Each book you write will make the next book at least a little bit easier. While it's good to share ideas with a wide audience, and better yet, if it can help pay the bills, writing a book is about more than sales.

The process of writing a book is useful. It can help you order thoughts, develop self-discipline, boost self-esteem and capture your words for future generations. It can also help you clear ideas from your head, perhaps allowing space for fresh ones to appear.

Different books can serve different purposes. You could choose to write a short eBook while you are first learning about creating eBooks, so you can learn about formatting with a small amount of text. You might write a short story anthology to test ideas you have for future novels, gather together stories you've written for competitions, or give people a taster of your writing style. You could write a book as a fundraiser for a charity. You might choose to develop a novel over many years to allow yourself time to research and hone it, in the hopes of becoming a literary name. You could write a book for nothing more than self-expression and therapy: the act of writing can be calming in itself.

Which books succeed is about luck and marketing. Don't be disappointed if this book doesn't top the charts. You may not get attention until your fifth book – or fiftieth. It might never happen. But there's always a chance that your book will resonate with people, and your stories could help change the world. If nothing else, writing a book helps you tick something off your bucket list. And if you want to write another book, you know what to do. Good luck writing your book. You can start now.

∞

About the Author

Emily Goss is an author and journalist who's also spent many years arranging art and science events, including Brighton Science Festival and art installations at Latitude Festival. First published aged 19 in a poetry anthology, she became a journalist in 1994 and an author in 2005. Since then, she's written over 30 books for publishers including Penguin Random House, Piatkus, Quiver and Hodder & Stoughton, and had titles translated into languages including French, Italian, Polish, Spanish, Dutch and German, as well as writing books for UK and US publishers. She also wrote and presented a show on Audible.com for a year. Her last book was Go Wild: Over 200 Ways to Connect With Nature, which she chose to self-publish as she wanted to keep the price as low as possible and have the option to give it away, to make it accessible to everyone.

Emily has written for TV, radio, film and publications ranging from the Guardian to The Lancet and Diva to Cosmopolitan. Most recently, after becoming increasingly disabled by Ehlers Danlos Syndrome, and associated health conditions, she founded Ciadish.co.uk – a website about books by Chronically Ill and Disabled writers, with reviews, interviews, features and writing opportunities. She also runs nature, arts and crafting and eco website, GrowEatGift.com for fun. Her next book is a novel about the women of the Arts and Crafts movement, focusing on May and Jane Morris, along with a fictional working class heroine – if she can find a publisher. If not, that will be self-published too. Follow her on BlueSky @BarrowMember.

Printed in Great Britain
by Amazon